Nipper

Peter Massam

BALBOA.PRESS
A DIVISION OF HAY HOUSE

Copyright © 2022 Peter Massam.

All rights reserved. No part of this book may be used or reproduced by any means, graphic, electronic, or mechanical, including photocopying, recording, taping or by any information storage retrieval system without the written permission of the author except in the case of brief quotations embodied in critical articles and reviews.

Balboa Press books may be ordered through booksellers or by contacting:

Balboa Press
A Division of Hay House
1663 Liberty Drive
Bloomington, IN 47403
www.balboapress.co.uk
UK TFN: 0800 0148647 (Toll Free inside the UK)
UK Local: (02) 0369 56325 (+44 20 3695 6325 from outside the UK)

Because of the dynamic nature of the Internet, any web addresses or links contained in this book may have changed since publication and may no longer be valid. The views expressed in this work are solely those of the author and do not necessarily reflect the views of the publisher, and the publisher hereby disclaims any responsibility for them.

The author of this book does not dispense medical advice or prescribe the use of any technique as a form of treatment for physical, emotional, or medical problems without the advice of a physician, either directly or indirectly. The intent of the author is only to offer information of a general nature to help you in your quest for emotional and spiritual well-being. In the event you use any of the information in this book for yourself, which is your constitutional right, the author and the publisher assume no responsibility for your actions.

Any people depicted in stock imagery provided by Getty Images are models, and such images are being used for illustrative purposes only. Certain stock imagery © Getty Images.

Print information available on the last page.

ISBN: 978-1-9822-8607-1 (sc)
ISBN: 978-1-9822-8609-5 (hc)
ISBN: 978-1-9822-8608-8 (e)

Balboa Press rev. date: 07/11/2022

Contents

Preface ix
Series xi
Other Publications xiii

A la Recherche du Paradis 1
Show us your moneybox 5
Life Balance 11
Restoring the Balance 17
First Encounter 23
Per Ardua ad Alta 27
Second Encounter 33
Repercussions 41
Late Developer 47
Third Encounter 55
Work Experience 61
Everything in Moderation 77

About the Author 87

For Jean

Preface

It is curious how our early experiences mould our actions, reactions and expectations of what is to come.

It is curious how the first book to make a solid impression on this author as a small boy was not the unimaginably turgid first two pages of *A Tale of Two Cities* – most unwisely thrust in his hands at the tender age of seven by his grandmother, from which he truly never recovered – but was many years later from *La Gloire de Mon Père* by Marcel Pagnol, written entirely in French. That book lauds the small things which parents do and what family life achieves, against the background of the sights and sounds of the French countryside which became familiar to their son. Long after the final page is turned the scent of the *maquis* and the sound of the *perdrix* linger on.

This first, small volume gives an account of how one boy, George, grows up in the safety of a spartan but loving home, and how freedoms are afforded so easily to those who have so little.

Part of that growing up is the introduction into the life equation of encounters with girls, younger and older. Haunted by the spectre of his first school bus journey to "big school" and the scars it left, his suppressed tears make him incandescent with pent-up rage, which he carried well into later life.

This is the story of how one boy's opinion was turned and how a young man's expectations were raised and confounded in equal measure, emerging from the experience with his second most memorable book – a keepsake from a third encounter of the feminine kind.

Series

This volume forms part of a trilogy series:

> *Nipper*
> *Moose Conquering Fear*
> *Know Your Mind*

    They track a lifetime journey of learning experiences from childhood encounters through coming of age to conquering fear, which culminate in a new appreciation of the power of the mind in the realms of communication, pain relief and self-help healing and preservation.

Other Publications

Also by Peter Massam:

Customer Experience

Managing Service Level Quality across Wireless and Fixed Networks (2002)
ISBN–13: 978–0470848487

First Cuz Collection of Poems

Sketch Poems (2019; Audible 2020)
ISBN–13: 978–1701299238

Second Cuz Collection of Poems

Reflections in a Country Garden (2021)
ISBN–13: 979–8723096103

We spend much of our life looking for the one we can't live without... and then have to find a way to do just that.

A la Recherche du Paradis

Two boys settle down on the grass verge of a small village green, a nervous glance at each other confirms the butterflies being suppressed within. A lie – perhaps the first subterfuge – had been played on one boy's mother only minutes before. Ignoring the curiosity from a bewildered but caring maternal look, George hurried out of the back door clutching the now full, plastic washing-up liquid bottle, hastily filled at the kitchen sink with cold water. Rounding the corner along the short curved path, he'd spotted Andrew already installed by the roadside with his own bottle at the ready.

'This'll be fun.' George said through a half-open mouth, wanting his friend to hear but no one else.

'I've saved the best place for us.' Andrew exclaimed in a much louder voice.

'What? You've done this before?'

'Only once or twice, but never up this end of the village before. Quick, sit down next to me and hide the bottle between your knees. No one will ever know.'

Happy to follow orders from an "old hand" made George more relaxed at first and less tense about what had seemed to be at least a mild transgression, but which now was compounded by the uneasiness of lying to a parent, turning it more into an inadvisable misdeed. The discomfort never left his eyes throughout.

'Look out! Here comes one now.' Andrew bellowed, causing his friend to glance backwards over their shoulders to see if any of the adjacent house windows bordering the green were open. After all, it was summer but the hour nearing lunchtime meant that most would be inside preparing food... with any luck.

Leaning forward past Andrew to get a better view meant George's head was protruding out into the road. Before he knew it, a horn blasted in his ears as a car raced past before pulling up at the T-Junction, no more than 20 metres from where they sat.

'That was a close shave!' George said.

'Lucky for us we had our legs tucked up on the bank, otherwise it could have been a lot worse.' replied his genuinely concerned friend, 'I'll lean back a bit so you have a clearer view next time.'

No sooner had the words left Andrew's lips than a second car appeared from nowhere; hearts were now thumping inside them both.

'Here we go!' screamed Andrew even more loudly than before.

'OK,' retorted George, 'let's give it all we've got!' with just as much gusto now as his friend.

With an impulsive but instinctive squeeze of the bottles, cold water with remnants of washing-up liquid shot out at the side of the passing car. They gave it both barrels, making an audible liquid-against-metal noise that they both heard clearly. A sudden, instantaneous thought occurred to them both, tuned in to each other's wavelength perfectly.

'Cripes! What if the driver heard it too?'

Before either had time to think, the blinding glare of red brake lights reflected on both their clothes. Not waiting for the car door to open, they leapt to their feet and ran like mad, off down the road to the nearest side lane which it would be difficult to follow in a car... but on foot, for sure. So they kept running, past the new houses' back gardens, along leafy paths, dry underfoot thank goodness, jumping over obstacles carelessly left by lazy fridge owners or settee sitters, who jettisoned items deprived of love or care.

Arriving out of breath at the lower end of the village, a pause was in order. Furtive looks cast all around them towards all and any entrance from which a pursuer could emerge kept their hearts racing. Thirst grabbed them by the throat at the same time, followed swiftly by the realisation that both had abandoned their respective bottles at the scene of what was increasingly looking like a crime.

'How am I going to explain that one away to my Mum?' George bleated.

'Think we'd better head home.' consoled Andrew in a more contrite voice, 'See you tomorrow.'

Of all the people George had met, he felt that Andrew was the first person to understand him and let them grow together.

Even more surprising was it then, when Andrew missed one, then two and more days off school. Having personally missed the first two years off school through a spate of perpetual illnesses, this didn't strike George as odd: he just wished his friend would get better soon.

As days turned into weeks, George was prompted to ask the question at home, to see if the adults knew how he was doing.

'Oh,' came the nonchalant reply, 'they had to move out of the village.'

'Move out of the village? Who does that?' George asked bewilderingly of his mother. No earthly responses could explain this away; other replies were simply not heard by George.

'Gone where? Another planet?' he thought to himself. 'What is there outside this village? This world I knew my way round and everyone in it, pretty much.' George wondered.

Taking this change on board took what seemed like forever. Finding another Andrew would take another ten years when George himself would flee the village.

For now there was school, which continued with much to catch up on, to keep his mind occupied until the day another bombshell dropped.

Show us your moneybox

At the lower end of the village, where Andrew and George had come to rest that day, lived one set of George's grandparents in a red-brick house alongside many others, which fanned out almost in a circle around a crescent on a road with the same name.

Visits there were filled with anticipation. The house and particularly the garden were larger than at George's house, where he could run around to his heart's content; plenty of grass and more importantly plenty to eat from the garden. He tasted his first carrots there and learnt the name of his first favourite apple, small but perfectly formed, cloaked in autumnal red and orange completely across its surface, with the rather grand-sounding name: Cox's Orange Pippin.

The garden consisted of two vegetable and fruit tree parcels; a plot separated by an evergreen grass path lush enough to lay among the blades without being prickled or stung; the gardener who tended to this large plot was an extraordinary man.

George first caught sight of him standing, legs stretched apart with hoe in hand, weeding his runner beans and carrots. Although George couldn't make out what he said from afar, he seemed annoyed with the weeds at his feet, but on George's approach he lifted his head up and beamed a broad smile in his direction.

'Enough of this nipper. What do you say, we go on inside and see what's to eat. Maybe we'll find a special treat waiting there for you too.'

To George's ears this was heaven: an adult who made a point of speaking directly with everyone. George would gladly have stayed outside, as on other occasions, chatting till the air turned chilly enough to seek shelter inside. But for now, he was hungry. So in he went.

The three brick steps into the kitchen were possibly the steepest George had ever encountered; how he wished that every measurement taken against the kitchen wall next to the door jamb would make him tall enough to climb those steps more easily.

He hurried quickly through the kitchen to lessen the cold impact of the scullery tiles on the thinning soles of his school sandals.

Passing in front of the permanently closed curtain covering the front door, which no one seemed to use, he moved on into the main room. It had a large, expansive window giving out onto a side garden with what seemed like rambling roses, forming clusters of bushes in an untidy grove.

His eyes scanned the room for anything new or anything which could potentially be eaten or constitute a treat, but nothing stood out. The table was clear and the Welsh dresser was adorned with its usual turquoise and black china tea cups, neatly hanging, equally spaced out under shelves and plates with the same design perched above them, some more precariously than others.

He took up his customary position at the end nearest the door and its draught, furthest from the fire which was rarely lit. Enter left his grandmother, who was not greeted as she often repeated the request for children to be seen and not heard – a message burned into every child's brain at that time, putting George and his peers squarely in the roles of observer.

As the talk was not directed at him, he let the words wash over him oblivious to all but the necessary manners to adhere to, awaiting the arrival of the erstwhile gardener extraordinaire and now most cherished grandfather.

The latter did not disappoint. He had never liked his grandson's name which oozed formality and pretentious, pseudo-royalty too much and at an early stage decided to call him 'Sammie'. No one questioned this, least of all Sammie's parents. Besides, most of their other sons and daughters, Sammie's aunts and uncles that is, seemed to go by different pseudonyms to their actual Christian names: John was known as Jim; his son was Jimmy, which made it easier to remember who belonged to whom at a group Sunday lunch, where more than thirty adults and children had convened; then there was David Charles who also went by the name of Sammie, but he had sadly died at Arnhem, so this Sammie never got to meet him.

George had wondered if there might be a special association in being referred to as Sammie, ever since his mum, with eyes welling up, and her mother with unremitting grimace and a hint of resentment had pointed out an uncanny resemblance between George's photo taken at primary school and that of the last photo taken of Sammie in his glider pilot's uniform before he left. The older photo was quite different of course – between the darker background and the almost cream-coloured uniform, there emanated a warm candour through the lighter sepia colours of his broad-smiling face and generous hands. 'A handsome chappie,' said Nan, 'But such a mischief too. Nothing but trouble!'

George's mum remained silent, wiping an escaped tear from the corner of one eye.

So 'Sammie' it was to be in that house to his closest family of aunts, uncles and cousins, while he was George to the outside world. To his grandfather it sounded more friendly, which was just the way they both wanted it.

Making his way steadily, but in a somewhat laboured manner to the seat next to where Sammie was standing, his grandad lowered himself carefully into his chair. The chill from the door increased as someone else entered the kitchen through the back door. For some while the other adults conversed, referring to the children obliquely and certainly not dwelling too long on them, for fear of upsetting the family equilibrium.

Only on the occasions when all nine "adult children" family members were together, did the mood lighten and change – when a total of 27 cousins descended on some Sundays to all be together. Then the garden, which extended on three sides of the house, was their treasure trove to explore, their natural playground where all fruit trees were scalable and where life's adventures began.

If the weather was inclement, then indoors was the only option where his nan would regale them all by repeating one of her many stories which older cousins knew off by heart. Sammie's favourite concerned his grandad retiring to the kitchen to wash up after a roast lunch. Nan was very proud of her recent purchase of a new frying pan with a non-stick surface, which she had used for the first time that morning to prepare the meal. As people's meals were digesting and the children were sent out to play, she began to wonder why grandad was taking so long in the kitchen. She called out several times to him, breaking up the conversation with 'Are you done yet?', 'We're waiting on you to start a game' and 'What the devil are you up to?' This continued for a good thirty minutes or so before grandad appeared at the main room door, his chest puffed out and declaring his success.

'What success are you talking about?' said Nan.

'Well, it took me a while but I wouldn't let it beat me' he announced.

'What do you mean?'

'That new pan of yours: it took some doing but with a lot of iron wool I got the pan clean eventually, and it's not black on the inside anymore!'

The roars of laughter could be heard even from outside at this tale of new technology, a non-stick pan, being beaten by sheer brute force and Australian determination to see a job through.

Sammie's parents had come through the kitchen into the main room and were about to take their leave, when grandad piped up that he'd promised the nipper a treat and asked if he could just take five minutes to do that. Sammie's heart leapt to think he hadn't forgotten, like other parents and grandparents did when other things somehow got in the way.

He invited Sammie to climb up onto his knee and sat him down squarely across both legs. Perhaps because of the door being left open, Sammie still felt a chill even though he was now perched on his grandad, but tried to put it out of his mind. 'Now for the treat, my lad,' he said, 'would you like to see Grandad's moneybox?'

The only moneybox Sammie had was very compact, enough to hold a year's worth of pocket money, which could then be used to buy some carefully selected presents – always the same every year: Turkish delight for Nan, nougat for Grandad and stem ginger for Dad. Not enough to buy Mum a present, but hugs aplenty for her made Sammie feel he had done his bit.

'Yes please Grandad.' Sammie exclaimed excitedly. He reached down one trouser leg and hoisted it halfway up his leg to reveal a hole about the size of a crown, which Sammie had only ever heard about though never seen, in a copper-coloured tin leg. 'That's where I keep all my money.' he whispered close to Sammie's ear. Sammie's expression showed complete disbelief but at once admiration for such a cunning hiding place. Only years later would he understand how he had lost both his legs in two world wars and still survived with such infectious humour.

Life Balance

Given permission to ride back home, George – back as his other worldly self – mounted his repainted silver and grey bike and braced himself for the ride back along the pathways which linked the two homes. It wasn't that the paths themselves were not smooth enough to make the ride enjoyable, but the solid tyres turned every stone hit or minor dip encountered into a major obstacle. This threatened to unseat its rider or, at the very least, cause considerable pain to the buttocks daring to rest on the saddle at those moments. With experience, George had learned to ride out of the saddle for most of the short journey back home.

'Everything comes at a price' he had once heard someone say. Well, sitting by the edge of the same road where the washing-up liquid squirting incident had taken place, he contemplated momentarily how he was ever going to afford to buy a car. He had seen the price on the cover of a car magazine. When comparing it to the pocket money he received each week, the challenge seemed undeniably impossible. He quickly dismissed it from his thoughts, returning to the small dust bowl on one end of the small village green nearest to his house, where he carried on playing with his paint-battered, worldly-wise, solid toys. It was within easy earshot of his house. While his voice hummed low engine drones to accompany the construction works in the dust bowl, he kept one ear open and alert to the most welcome words of all which beckoned him in their direction: 'Tea's ready'.

He gathered up his lead digger and lorry and hurried on inside. Tea was always brief, as the call of the outside was unceasing.

'Man cannot live by bread alone' was a popular echo heard from many adults, usually on a Sunday, on returning from church (though not all attended, it must be said). 'Well, if it always had strawberry jam spread on it,' thought George, 'I would think that entirely possible.'

'Please may I get down from the table?' George recited, knowing that refusal of such politeness was almost unheard of, and compliance sure to achieve his aim. On the back lawn – no bigger than a handkerchief – stood a sizeable pond embedded in it, which required constant attention. He hurried to the edge to peer down into its dark depths. 'The goldfish might be hungry, Georgie.' his father suggested, appearing from his shed with blades and sharpening stone in hand. George needed no further invitation, as this entailed a short crossing of the road to the much larger blacksmith's pond opposite their house. In fact the blacksmith used to live in their house, he was told, which was why the house stood so proud of the surrounding land by a good twelve inches or more. With centuries of discarded ash turning the soil around the house into a fertile market garden, a nursery had been created by his father for all manner of vegetables seeing their first light of day, before being transplanted into larger spaces in the allotments further away.

To feed the fish required no trip to a pet store as everything was on hand and George had the right tool for the job, thanks to the ingenuity of his father and full co-operation of his mother.

The fishing net consisted of a cane with a circular wire inserted at one end, by bending the two ends of the wire at right angles. Their springiness ensured they remained in place while the net was being used. This would have looked like any other homemade net but for the net itself, designed so cunningly to capture the very small red creatures called daphnia.

Their goldfish – indeed any fish – loved them... although he couldn't vouch for the solitary catfish that had been talked about many times, but had never put in an appearance. He often imagined it to be a dragon-like, almost an Arthurian creature of legend, stalking the murky bottom, sifting through the mud with its long barbs.

Without the finest of meshes, an ordinary net would just let the daphnia pass through. So the material for this was critical to the success of this 'fishing trip' and that's where his Mum's stockings came in. While never quite understanding how his mother could go through so many pairs of stockings, she was nevertheless always willing to provide George with a newly discarded pair, should they ever develop a hole. Threading the wire through the top of the stocking was a well-practised art for George, as was cutting and tying it off in a knot, learnt from the one adult whose seemingly unquenchable ability to solve any problems knew no bounds – his dad.

Armed with a newly refurbished net, he set off across the road to the preferred shady spot underneath the willow tree.

It cast its dappled shadows over the clear, slightly red-coloured water, betraying the daphnia's presence and abundance. With slow sweeps from left to right and back again, the net was soon bulging with the intensely blood-red masses. The fish would not go hungry tonight!

Skipping back across the road with the net laden, supporting it underneath with one of his hands, George upended the contents into the small pond, where the daphnia found new freedom briefly before the goldfish sensed their presence and ate their fill.

Sometimes when daphnia were scarce, a short walk around the corner into The Bailey was necessary. It was an undulating field of short-cropped grass, occasional nettle clumps and dips, which often filled with water from overnight rain, the grass laying still on the surface until wellies disturbed the surface. Elm trees dotted the landscape in a disorderly fashion. They provided perfect shelter from the Friesian cows below, that were only too willing to devour the twigs and small branches of leaves that George and his friends threw down from their vantage point. For the cows, it probably relieved the boredom of eating nothing but grass all day; for the boys, it was a chance to hone their tree-climbing skills and take in a bird's eye view of the surrounding village.

Some of the larger ponds there housed similar underwater flurries of the red gold that was daphnia, but that required sure footing on the steeper banks to avoid an early muddy bath. Villagers often passed through as a shortcut or to walk their dogs. George supposed that they also were sent to keep an eye on the wild children, who frequently returned with mud up to their knees and wellies brimming over with smelly pond water.

For the less fortunate households, the boy returned with only one trainer, the other left stranded where the cows went down to the water's edge to drink, in one of the boggy holes they left behind. There was no mistaking that smell!

When there was a gap in his helpful tasks, George liked nothing better than to use his newly found skill of riding a bike to shoot off down to the "rec". With the air rushing past his ears and seemingly endless routes to take through the village, he found new pleasure on the wide paths and tracks, expanding his horizons as far as the recreation ground. There awaited the dual delights of football with his mates and play equipment, dwarfed by an enormous, shiny metal slide.

Early on in his use of the slide, George became quickly aware of the secrets of applying candle wax on metal. This made the ride even more exhilarating, propelling both him – and some unsuspecting newcomers to the village – well beyond the natural end of the slide into a dusty hollow, frequently dumping them on their rears.

There was, it seemed to George, no end to the amount of pleasure to be had in this village.

Until, that is, the day that a lull in these distractions prompted George to ask 'It's a long time since we've been to Nan and Grandad's. When can we go next to see them?' The innocence of the remark visibly took his mother aback. However, after almost two years, the inevitability of it did not.

The painful truth had to be shared finally, which totally consumed his tender ten years in an instant, projecting him early into adulthood in the cruellest of ways.

'When did he pass away?' he sobbed, taking forced gulps of air between each word. New words and new emotions came in waves and knocked him to the floor. 'Nearly two years ago?' he muttered angrily in disbelief, 'why didn't you tell me before now?'

Explanations long or short held no sway over George, who shrunk inside himself, harbouring anger and even hatred for the first time towards his parents. The realisation that he had been excluded from the funeral and never given a chance to say his goodbyes, while everyone else did, was overwhelming.

The gravity of that moment felt like a landslide inside, taking great swathes of his innocence with it, from which he never really recovered. A world without his grandad was unimaginable.

Restoring the Balance

There were many silences after that day; there followed a disinterest in the mundane things like school homework; tasks became chores and pleasures hard to find or enjoy.

Returning one summer's day after school, he found his mother in a not unfamiliar pose at the ironing board. George slumped down into the armchair next to the unlit fire, which gave out a perpetual smell of damp coal waiting for the first cold night to be reignited.

He was staring intently out of the window a good few feet above him, as the sitting room floor lay below the window ledge line. The late afternoon's sun's rays streaming through the net curtains captured his gaze. His mother, seeing his now familiar glum and tired face, mentioned nonchalantly, 'Be careful how you sit down on that chair now.' George looked puzzled, in her direction for once.

'There's a little surprise for you.'

'Surprise? What surprise?'

'Well just look for yourself.'

He looked under as far as he could by leaning over the edge, but saw nothing. 'Are you sure there's a surprise under here?' he challenged.

'Look further,' came the response, 'seek and you shall find.'

Sliding off the edge of the armchair seat cushion slowly onto the hard floor covered by a well-worn carpet, he turned to face the pale green sitting room wall and lowered his head till it almost touched the floor. There, at the very back of that space was a tiny puppy, afraid to come out it seemed but wagging its tiny white tail enthusiastically when it saw George. An instant bond had been formed.

'He's all yours George,' she said softly, 'but you'll have to look after him, take him for walks and teach him good manners and other things.'

The most noticeable feature of his new found friend – and later his confidant – were the two distinctive black patches over both his eyes.

'What shall we call him, George?' to which the reply came back immediately, 'Why, Patch, of course!'

'Patch it is then.'

These patches stood out on what was otherwise a mostly white body.

'What type is he?' George inquired.

'A cross between a Beagle and a Dalmatian and what's more... his brother is down at Nan's.'

This was even more exciting. Brothers from the same dog family, only a stone's throw away from each other. 'Can we go and see his brother and introduce them?' George asked animatedly, 'I bet they'll be surprised to see each other.'

The short trip took longer than usual as the journey was far too long for one so small, so he had to be carried all the way. Once there his brother, named Jimmy, jumped out of his nan's arms at the sight of Patch. Jimmy had more Dalmatian in him:

you could tell from the amount of spots on his body. Goodness, he was lively, bounding around Patch, small as they both were, with Patch looking bewildered, wondering what had got into his brother. It was a scene to savour and one that was repeated often on weekends and some evenings too.

The crescent where Jimmy lived had a large circular green at its centre, which was ample space for the youngster to race around, but once he grew in stature he started to venture further afield. The crescent joined the bottom road at a T-Junction, which is where Jimmy met an untimely end. A life cut short in his dog year youth. George felt sure Patch would feel the loss and gave him extra hugs for weeks to lessen the pain.

Patch would go on to become George's lifelong friend of seventeen and a half human years, holding the fort long after George had left for and returned from university. He memorised his two regular walks so well, that even failing sight, deafness and aching limbs could not deter him from following them daily. Eventually he was taken to the vet's as a kindness, after he was found wandering aimlessly around the garden and a great friendship and companionship drew to a close. George still remembers him fondly to this day.

One such memory was Patch's lack of understanding of the concept of the game of hide and seek. It took place on a wonderful tree-covered mount, which once formed part of a motte and bailey at the heart of the village. It seemed like a mountain adventure to George and his peers. The hill was interlaced with overgrown pathways, almost surrounded by water on three sides and was covered in deep undergrowth. Significantly, it housed their own excavation tunnel into the chalk hillside, where all manner of games and film scenes were re-enacted.

So thick was the tree cover on this hill, that the village seemed glad that its young residents took to chopping down the smaller trees in late October and early November, to be hauled the short distance to another village green nearby, where the annual bonfire took place. When axes were not the order of the day, more traditional games like hide and seek were played and Patch played his part. George's pursuers soon learnt that it was easy to find him. They just had to tell Patch to 'Find George!' and follow his trail straight to where George was hiding. 'You're hopeless!' smiled George, as he cuddled Patch again and congratulated him on being so clever at this game.

Another game he was good at was football. The recreation ground was vast and the surrounding borders were completely wild with ditches on one side, allotments on another and open cow fields on the others. These fascinating edges occupied Patch for much of the friends' friendly game of football. Just as the boys were starting to tire or become weary of the same players excelling where others could not, Patch would appear from nowhere and dribble the ball between his two front paws at lightning speed towards the opponents' goal with startling accuracy. They all collapsed about laughing and agreed amicably that it was time to end the game.

Patch didn't always rely on his own steam to speed along the small roads of the village, especially going down the main street to the allotments at the bottom end of the village. There, George's father tended diligently two or three times a week to half an acre of land, which provided their family of five with fresh vegetables, fruit and the staple that was the humble potato.

Harvesting potatoes was a two-stage affair: Digging them out of the ground was the first of these. It was always fascinating never being able to guess the exact number or size of potatoes that would be revealed, when digging into the heaped up rows beneath the yellowing leaves and stems. The second stage was gathering them together, rubbing the earth from them and placing them carefully into a clamp. This seemed almost to mirror the Anglo-Saxon dwelling George had learned about at school. Mounds of unblemished potatoes, covered with layers of fresh straw and topped off with a generous helping of earth, making sure there was a straw chimney at the very top to allow the sleeping vegetables to breathe.

As the winter progressed, it was down to George and his father to break open these clamps one at a time, retrieve the still immaculate potatoes and place them in sacks, ready for transporting back up the hill on a man-made trolley. This was no steel framed castoff or sequestered supermarket trolley, but another ingenious reuse of materials no longer needed by a growing family. With the need for a pram long passed, it was disassembled and the wheels – two large at the rear and two small for the front steering mechanism – were attached to a sturdy wooden frame and secured expertly by the soon-to-be craftsman engineer that was George's father.

Half sitting and half kneeling on the back of the trolley, George pushed the ground away from him with one foot, propelling it along the flat start of the journey from his house. Before long though, the main street took a steep dive down a forever slope. George turned to face forwards, stretching out his limbs in front of him, to steer with his feet. It was at this point that Patch jumped on, between George's legs and sniffed the air as it raced past his nostrils.

Passing the same friend's house more than half way down – where the slope was at its steepest – was the signal for George to stick both feet out and down onto the ground to slow the cart down a touch, as it careered past parked cars to the right of them. Such was the lightness of the traffic that the sharp bend to the left at the bottom never encountered any moving cars or other obstacles. This gave them a clear run for another hundred metres to the small, grassy incline leading to the allotment entrance, where the trolley came to rest.

George disembarked, exhilarated, along with Patch who had other corners to explore. The return journey would see the trolley loaded up with two to three sacks and no room for passengers, but there was always next time!

First Encounter

There were many 'next times' but these became fewer and farther between as George's journeying switched to motorised transport, of the 'school bus' variety.

The importance of education for their whole family had always been the main aim of George's parents and in his turn, George followed in the footsteps of his siblings – though very much later than them – in attending a 'big school'. He had been warned also that there would be girls on the bus too. This did not faze him in the least. He had an elder sister, who had always looked after her "little bruv". By and large the girls and boys at primary school got on well with each other too, with one or two exceptions. For example, he found it odd how the only girl he had wanted to talk to at the school, chose the sportiest boy as her pseudo-boyfriend. However, George did at least get to play opposite her in the lead roles of the last play performed there in their last year. A consolation prize perhaps and proof that there is a just world out there after all.

The lead up to that first day had been long and protracted. George's Mum had saved hard, dividing the weeks' wages as always between the necessities of life in little boxes made of standard hardboard, which sat as a 4 x 3 set of drawers painted white on the mantelshelf in their bedroom. Categories had been etched by hand in black ink onto the white painted hardboard with some mistakes carefully redrawn. Coal, Elec, Water, Food among others, with a drawer that was marked Saving… which was always empty.

Having no notion of what things cost, George only knew that what few arguments there were in the house seemed to relate to money and in his case, the cost of the uniform. He didn't mind looking a bit odd and had come to expect that his trousers, and even the jacket, would be too long and large for him. That made perfect sense. But the need for a cap eluded his reasoning and, in spite of remonstrations to the contrary by him, his parents decided it would be for the best to have one, so as not to look out of place. Their sense of dignity was in George's best interests. He knew that now.

With the day upon him, he rose earlier than ever before to down his breakfast and struggle with the new uniform. His Mum was indispensable in helping him with his tie – another strange convention – whose sole purpose seemed to be a steady but slow death by strangulation.

It was only a brief walk to the place where the bus stopped. The morning was fresh with autumn hastening on, sending a cold draught across the legs of all who were waiting. Some shuffled from one foot to another to keep warm in the early morning dew, which had formed on the grassy verge where they were forced to wait. For George, he was simply glad not to be in short trousers any more. He didn't care if his long trousers were longer than long. They were keeping him warm.

FIRST ENCOUNTER

The bus pulled up and they took their seats. As a new boy, George chose a free seat with no one else in it, as he did not recognise anyone on the bus.

The bus paused with its engine running and the heater humming. George wiped at the condensation on the window to take a look at the butcher's garden immediately to his right, wondering what new things he would learn today, what the new school would be like, the masters and the boys. In his dreamlike state, he had omitted to remove his cap. The bus door opened to a late influx of a small group of two boys and one girl, who belatedly made their way noisily down the central aisle; one knocked his cap off and a hand grabbed a full handful of hair on his head and pulled it hard… and again… and harder still.

Fearing that he might lose all of that hair, he froze and wished the pain would stop. But it continued as tears welled up in his eyes. He fought back the tears, but they came all the same. Excruciating pain such as this he had never experienced. As quickly as it has started, the hand released its vicelike grip and made its way to the back of the bus, where it received admiring congratulations: 'Nice one!' laughed the group in unison.

From their loud and raucous excitement, George managed to hear the name Lynn. Unsure as to who this was, he stole a glance backwards briefly to the back of the aisle and realised that that awful act had come from a she. 'So this is what I can expect from girls, is it?' he thought to himself and resolved from that day forward to have nothing to do with them.

Per Ardua ad Alta

Fortunately for him, the school he was about to attend for the next seven years was an all-boys school. He breathed a small sigh of relief after that incident, but it was one that stayed with him for several weeks of bus journeys, for fear of repetition. Luckily their attention was easily distracted and it never recurred. However, the blight of girls remained with him and excepting his sister, who was the very epitome of kindness, the rest of female humanity passed him by only too willingly.

That included the sister school on the hill, to which many of his older peers spent increasing amounts of time repairing to at lunchtime. 'What's got into them?' he thought on more than one occasion, 'Don't they care to eat?' he pondered, quite mystified by their behaviour, 'Lunches were not all that bad.' Even as he approached his teenage years, when all his hormones are said to be racing, girls did not figure in the grand world equation.

Of course the word 'hormones' was unknown to George and his generation because, between Religious Education and Biology, they managed to avoid the awkward relationship topics, preventing them from ever seeing the light of day. In fact there was only one Biology lesson George could recall, where a couple of enlightened sniggers – more enlightened that the 28 others in the class – were stifled by the diminutive biology master. He was a kindly spoken, short and somewhat rotund man – from his enjoyment of free lunches George always thought – who found talking about the basics of reproduction slightly embarrassing. He preferred to keep to the animal kingdom examples, before moving swiftly on to the more sensible hermaphrodite snails or to the vastly superior worms, who could replicate themselves... even when sliced in two! Much of the class spent many subsequent hours testing out that theory with some intensive, albeit all too brief, gardening at home.

To such heights were their minds raised in keeping with the ever-present school motto 'Per Ardua ad Alta', steering well clear of the depraved depths which would not be in keeping with the religious discipline: one which had forged the school all the way back in 1632.

'The best years of your life' echoed in George's ears from many different directions while growing up. 'Well, those people,' he thought, 'never had to sit through a history lesson!'

It was with enormous relief that just one year in, he had to choose between History and Geography and at the same time between Latin and German. 'No contest!' he declared and then mused bewilderingly, 'Why would anyone want to study a language so close to the end of a war with that country?' The decision to stick with Geography was rewarded much later, when the physical features of tarns, ribbon lakes, hanging valleys, glacial moraine and – God bless them – drumlins were revealed to the assembled class and they had to draw all of them.

That appealed much more than those confounded dates, which were constantly asked for, to be memorised and reproduced at will and at random. With no context to hang them on and no storyline to attach to them, History teaching by the "tank"– as he was affectionately known – was destined to be short-lived. Only decades later would George realise the importance of historical context in his own studies, which left him with an enormous gap in his understanding.

They weren't all happy days naturally. One particularly nasty year group, when George was in the junior school, made it their mission to terrorise the younger boys at playtime, disrupting their games and bullying groups rather than individuals. Only when George was in the same year as them, did he realise the pressures they are subjected to, which may have been a factor. However, a sixth form teacher confided to them in the later days at the school, that that particular year group had been problematical... and in a more extreme way than any other.

Even given the propensity for the human brain to extinguish the bad events in favour of the good ones, it seemed to George in quieter moments of contemplation, that there were many more enjoyable days and firm friendships than bad ones.

And then there was sport.

For a late developer such as George, sport did not figure largely to begin with. In fact, he struggled with many of the activities considered standard and necessary in a boys' school. Changing in less than two minutes he had under control, but climbing ropes, bench presses, throwing and catching medicine balls filled with sand were all beyond him. 'Why would anyone want to fill a ball with sand?' he pondered. He did not need convincing that he did not understand all the ways of this bewildering world.

Nor did he understand why Taffy, the PE teacher, was always referring to a pupil who never existed in their class, called John Thomas! He had to wait many more years before that explanation was unveiled to him, in what seemed like a succession of minor revelations, which a village boy was not privy to.

Much to his surprise though, as he approached his later teens, his body began to grow upwards, though hardly ever outwards. This afforded him some advantages in several sports, but put to best use on a hockey field, where everything was played at arm's length. Added to this physical change was the motivational change – required for any activity to be truly successful, while being immensely enjoyable at the same time – supplied by the then current coach of the men's national hockey team. The enthusiasm that man had for anyone of any shape, description or persuasion to become good at this, his sport, was nothing short of inspirational.

George was by no means a first team regular as he joined the party late, but he made good friends on the way, who invited him to join a local hockey club. The term "local" was relative of course: it was local for them, as they lived in the town just two miles away, but for George, it was to be a six mile bike trip there and back: a twelve mile round trip every Saturday during the season, and subsequently some Sundays too, for mixed games.

Two of the advantages of the sport became immediately apparent: firstly, his stamina and general physical strength improved immensely, when coupled with the biking to and fro every Saturday. It became less and less of a challenge, even climbing the steep contours to the intersection of the Icknield Way. Cycling became more of an enjoyable experience, a welcome distraction from the increasing amounts of studying that was being asked of him, and a chance to clear his head with fresh air.

The second advantage was the camaraderie between players, both within the men's teams and subsequently within the mixed teams on a Sunday. This engendered an increasing confidence under the startling realisation that he could, indeed, be good at sport. From that point, George was to undergo several revelations throughout his life in all manner of sports, which encouraged him to explore more, in an effort to become a more rounded sports person.

A third advantage, which only became apparent months and years later, was how much these excursions helped him be more outward looking, beyond the confines of a village boundary: just as a flower stem strikes out into the blue yonder with no sight of what lies ahead, but has the confidence from the warmth of the sun to rise higher and higher above its peers and competing plants, to open out into a delightful flower with a singular purpose.

So it was, he felt the sun's rays on his face or at his back as he cycled, which made him speed faster towards his destination with ease and delight for two purposes: one planned, to enjoy the company of friends after a gruelling match or encounter and two, unplanned, to make new friends of an altogether different nature.

Second Encounter

There was no escaping the fact that entering the sixth form was a life-changing event. Not only was the toil of studying nine different subjects put firmly behind him, but the change to smart casual clothing brought also a new release from conformity under uniform regulations. What's more, teachers of all his chosen three subjects treated them all like the adults they were longing to be.

Suddenly the talk before and after classes was more about life choices, issues facing society and life in general. The transformation over that summer was indeed liberating and the peculiar thing George found was that it had happened to every one of his peers too!

The world of work too was not far off and he had already had experience over Easter of fitting into a packing department of an electronics firm for four weeks. This was where his packing skills – hitherto pretty non-existent – were honed to perfection for any number of items. The parcels were protected against the perils of the postal service – royal or otherwise – and fitted into the smallest possible packaging for cost efficiency. Skills, he felt sure, which would remain with him for the rest of his days.

NIPPER

The meticulous attention to detail was impressed on him there too. His working area was opposite an intriguing cage, visited by next to nobody and permanently locked. Its shelves were covered in tiny cardboard boxes each with its own label and long number, stacked from ceiling to floor. The only variety of colour was provided by equally small trays of bright red, blue and yellow. 'Had they deliberately chosen primary colours?' he wondered during an unusually quiet five minutes, 'Or was there some other purpose for this rather regimental arrangement of treasured items.' The thought also passed through his mind that their caged worth perhaps belied their real value. He had heard that electronics components could contain gold. His imagination began to work overtime, before being brought back to earth with a bump, as several more orders needing to be fulfilled before the end of the day landed in front of him.

To his surprise, one order was from a government department and before he knew it, he was being given a run through of how fulfilment depended 100% on traceability of components and, at that point, he was introduced to the cage.

'Right down to every resistor and every diode!' exclaimed John, his mentor and tutor at the firm. A separate manual tabulated sheet had to be filled out, with many columns occupied by various long, impossible-to-memorise numbers and letters. 'Perhaps I'm destined to be part of the logistics arm for the secret service', George mused, before setting to work on completing the packaged order, ready for the afternoon collection.

Easter was a good time to work since the hockey season was all but over, except for the odd trip to Holland, where

SECOND ENCOUNTER

entertaining hundreds of hockey players for a week at a time was second nature to them.

It was towards the middle of a particularly cold February one year that George found himself covering for players off sick on a Sunday. This was the day designated for the incredibly challenging but rewarding sport that is mixed hockey. Never to be underestimated in terms of fun and commitment, it was still very competitive. In some cases more so than the men's game, where playing in the lower echelons was mostly about running and covering for one or two older colleagues, who found it hard to break into or sustain a run for more than a few seconds.

That Sunday, George found himself having to change shirts, not because an opponent had ripped it off his back, but because he had been asked to play for the opposition, who were desperately short of team members. He was reluctant to part with the thicker green home cotton shirt in favour of some flimsy black and crimson summer shirt, said to be 'the only spare' the opposition had. At any rate, the game continued and by the end of the game, he could no longer feel his hands due to the bitter cold: in some ways this could have been seen as a positive to numb incoming tackles, but the shock travelling up the stick was felt even more intensely when he mishit the ball. The result was immaterial as ever to most participants. More importantly, the fun and laughter reverberated long into the changing room afterwards. The entrance from there to the large bar area, where a few tables were scattered around the edge, was blocked by a voice. 'That was impressive!' it said, 'As was the change of strip midway through the game.'

Forced to look down to excuse himself so that he could pass through, he noticed shoulder-length hair couching a rounded face with a broad smile attached. 'Was this girl actually talking to him?' George thought. He had no time to respond before more of the same 'I didn't realise you played for the mixed team.'

'I only started this year.' offered George, still a little dumbstruck by the unusual happening. This was the first time this had happened to him. He had to think rapidly on his feet, as he'd surely known how to speak to his peers and his male teammates, but a girl ...

Fumbling for topics, he left for the tea that had been laid on and a drink found its way over to his table: a shandy, which always sent bubbles up his nose. He only hoped that his eyes did not water as they did on other occasions. Feeling still surprised at the encounter, he excused himself and slipped off to the toilets. On his return, he was taken aback again to find the same girl waiting to greet him, but this time the conversation began in a more earnest and open way, talking about pop music and other likes.

'Well I have to be getting back,' George excused himself again as he stood up, 'I have a six mile ride ahead of me.'

'Can I walk back with you, as I have to take the same road for a bit?'

'Of course.' he uttered, remembering the accepted practice of seeing a girl home, especially when the darkness drew in earlier.

So they left the building together and he saw her to her road before pushing off from the kerb with lightness, which he had not experienced before. He was oblivious to the undulations which floated effortlessly beneath his wheels.

'So that what's it's like to talk to a girl,' he said to the night air as he cycled home, 'without her grabbing great clumps of hair out from your head. Maybe there's something to this boy girl thing after all.'

Days passed – though not quickly enough – and another hockey weekend was upon him. The journey in was taking him less time and the hills became easier to negotiate, as another energy seemed to kick in now.

His private supporter did not disappoint him, showing up regularly pitch side, which did not escape the notice of George's peers from the school. The changing room banter in school turned towards him, somewhat unexpectedly.

'What about Moose then… you seem very close with that girl at the hockey club,' a fellow club player quizzed, 'what's the story with her?'

They wanted details – name, age, inside leg measurement – all the usual guff. George gave away the minimum to draw a shield around him, but they found another way in.

'Well, you've been seeing her that long… more than three weeks now… so you must be getting your leg over by now!' another nose interjected, to the amusement of all around.

'Well, that,' George stalled, 'I can't say,' trying to defend himself as well as his newly declared girlfriend by the assembled mass. He could feel his face redden and that uncomfortable feeling under his right armpit, which made him want to itch it interminably.

Fortunately the smell of Quinell's socks as he removed them diverted everyone's attention long enough for the inquisition to cease. At the same time the master called out for stragglers to get a move on and George's bacon was saved.

NIPPER

Time moved on and towards the end of the season, the partings between George and his girlfriend became a touch more intense in the kissing department. To the point where, after an end of year function at the club which went on till eleven o'clock or so, she invited him in to get warm before cycling back.

'Anything to drink? Warm drink that is?'

'Tea would be great.' he replied sitting down on the couch, 'So where are your parents?' George asked curiously, not wishing to disturb their peace.

'Oh, upstairs long ago. They're in bed.'

'Okay, I'll be quiet.' he whispered apologetically.

'No need,' she said confidently, 'they'll not bother us or come down now.'

The talking continued as she edged closer to him on the sofa, an arm reaching out in the direction of his leg, the other hand beginning to unbutton her blouse.

'Are you okay?' he asked in a concerned way.

'Yes sure,' came the reply, 'just a little hot, that's all.'

The two embraced long and hard for what seemed an eternity, much of it with his eyes closed – after all he had seen it done this way a few times on films he had been allowed to see – but when came the time to open them again he was stunned to see that she now lay beneath him, naked. This was his first time seeing breasts in the flesh, so he took in her small but well-formed pair and they continued to kiss passionately.

After what must have been ten minutes or more, she stirred from under him, lifted herself up from the couch and started to put her clothes back on.

SECOND ENCOUNTER

This perplexed George for a second, but as he had no clue as what to do next, he too got up, still fully clothed and made his way to the door. Taking his leave, he mounted his bicycle and rode home.

This was unknown territory.

Who could he confide in? Parents, certainly not; schoolmates, absolutely out of the question, the ridicule would go round the school like wildfire; friends from the village, no way, same response. There was no one. He was on his own with this one.

Repercussions

'What was it about girls?' he thought, 'Why can't things be simple; isn't there a guide to this stuff?'

It was less than a week later that he was surprised to bump into her again at their once usual meeting point outside a jewellers at lunchtime: a place on the public street with streams of boys, uniformed and otherwise, making their way "up the hill", which he knew now was code for going to meet girls coming out from the girls' school. From her demeanour and reluctance to look directly in George's general direction, he felt the conversation would not last very long. It didn't. It was just to say that she would be going down to Devon for a cricket festival, which he had never heard of. 'Funny how someone can sound more distant, as if they were on the phone rather than standing right in front of you', he puzzled to himself.

'For how long?'

'Oh,' she said nonchalantly, 'it lasts for three weeks.'

Knowing that this meant most of August, leaving precious little time before the normal back-to-school mania which took place between late August and early September, he was surprised at the length of time but thought no more of it.

'Alright. See you when you get back.'

She turned on her heels and marched off away from the town centre, presumably to a bus that would take her the two miles home.

As he walked back towards the dining room to see if there was anything left for lunch, he began to reflect on this parting for the first time. What had it meant? Something had clearly changed, but he struggled to put his finger on it. He still had much to learn.

'The school back entrance meeting had been like talking to an art exhibit', he pondered at length. At once beautiful to look at, but was indifferent to spoken communication. That quiet contemplative connection you sometimes find in looking at a sketch or work of art that speaks to you was missing, conspicuous by its absence his English and General Studies teacher would have said. He realised that this was what he yearned for, or at least needed to be part of it, a meaningful relationship that is.

But where was he to find his William Blake? Who could possibly be the equal of such a visionary, first introduced to him by that same ever enthusiastic English mentor and General Studies tutor? Did such individuals still exist? Being two hundred years Blake's senior and having gone unrecognised for much of his life, George was left emptied by the task of finding his like again. Surely they were all six feet under!

All he craved was to find someone he could rejoice in spending time with, without the need to talk and not feeling awkward at the silences between them: someone who could see the beauty of a wet afternoon like Camille Pissarro. Granted though, that was in Paris, and that city struggles not to look its best at the worst of times.

He dismissed the search from his mind and sought solace in his General Studies scheduled for later that afternoon, where Goya's firing squad seemed to understand his predicament perfectly!

The repercussions were swift, as soon as the three weeks expired and a return to school premises coincided with a trip into the town.

After the pleasantries were dispensed with on her stay, which she thoroughly enjoyed telling him about, several times in the course of the first five minutes, she pronounced,

'I'm looking for something different.'

'Sounds as though you found it down in Devon', came the slightly bitter reply.

'Yes I did indeeeed', deliberately holding onto that pleased sound, while lifting her eyes heavenward to mull over memories in front of him. Her return to Earth was equally as fast as her pronouncement: George now seemed like a distant recollection of a ridiculous mistake.

He felt it too. Trying hard to write it off as a misencounter, a circumstantial chance, which would have never happened, had he not appeared from the toilet at that exact moment at the hockey club.

His mind turned back to a previous similar feeling he had had at primary school. His mind was cast unwillingly back to what he would now call a crush on Alison, whose blond hair he remembered with affection, as she stood playing opposite him in Sinbad the Sailor. He thought about the moments on stage: the bad impression she must have had of him, as he had to sing painfully out of tune – being the only chorister in the assembly of his age, he was thought to have the mastery to pull it off. Whether he did or not, he could not tell – but the audience laughed anyway; the good impression or not she may have had of them interacting for much of the play, before a final awkward kiss; his disappointment afterwards that school was ending so soon and they would be off to different schools for always.

'There was something missing on both occasions, I suppose.' he said out loud.

His mind was then cast back even further – perhaps trying to assimilate the increasing misery he was now feeling – to his very first job for the princely sum of £22.30 per week, given to him in a small brown envelope designed to keep notes and coins dry, but failing to do so. George had looked forward to earning his first money because he had come to realise that pocket money, as welcome and generous as it was at half a crown, was not going to help him pay for better presents for his whole family.

Off he had set down Oldbridge Lane, with the three-legged milkmaid's stool, walking past the farm where his good friend and farmer's son, Joel, had spent many a summer's day with him, immersed in the harvest.

His mood lightened as he recalled hanging on for dear life to the trailer rail, as the tractor tipped its load of wheat into a vast hopper in the grain shed. Strong enough to withstand the steadily inclining trailer hydraulics, its floor was revealed to be a shiny metallic light grey, clean enough to eat a meal from… or so it seemed.

Arriving at the field several others, numbering ten or a dozen at most, were already assembled. They were a variety of ages – none as young as George mind – young and older adults, the older predominantly being ladies. He noticed how brightly coloured their seats were that they had brought. These seasoned pickers knew what to expect: some had banana or orange crates to sit on; others had what appeared to be old Tupperware buckets doubling up as stools. He tried to gain some inside knowledge before the work began. So he approached a lady, about the same age as his mother or maybe a little less.

'Hello,' he offered by way of an opening, 'hope I've come to the right place.'

'Oh yes, dearie,' came the reply directly, 'just make sure you take a sack with you too.'

'Oh, is that for sitting on?'

'No, my dear. That's for when it rains!'

Puzzled by this reply, he did not have to wait long before the lady had shown him, with great dexterity, how an old jute sack could double up as a hood with a long back. She was absolutely right.

When the rain came, as it inevitably would, the sack kept their backs dry for sure, but what it did not stop was the direction of the wind. Once that changed on the fourth and fifth days he was there, the rain lashed at his cheeks and face unremittingly. It was hard to see the pea vines in front of him and they came now with great clods of earth attached, which made stripping them harder and more tiresome. He enjoyed the chatter between all of them, but the rain he could do without.

'There must be easier jobs', he presumed and decided not to return after two weeks of relentless rain.

That drenched feeling returned to his knees and boots even now. That soaked to his bones, wet through experience only dissipated when he returned to the warmth of an open hearth, with a helping hand from Mum to remove his wet clothes and wrap him in a warm blanket in front of the blazing coal fire.

His eyes refocussed on what was immediately in front and around him. He found not the worn, still bright blue and red vibrant seat covers beneath him in his front room, but instead, the dull yellows but welcoming greens of functional, educational armchairs.

His return to normality was helped in the sixth form centre by his mates' cheery disposition, which nothing outside those walls could faze or dare to impinge upon. Before he knew it, he was back for his final year and after a week's rest, was thinking wistfully to himself, 'Suppose it's just as well. I have loads to do this year and no end in sight as it stands.' With that, he extended his spine a little more that day, standing straighter and taller than those of his peers around him on the first day back. He had grown some more.

Late Developer

It was while he was becoming increasingly involved in sports, that George was heartened and uplifted to be told by his hockey master that not everyone develops at the same rate. This had given hope to someone convinced he would be confined to the side lines, cheering on others. This he had done on many occasions as he rarely made the first XI and did not expect to. George contented himself with the second XI and enjoyed the ride. He would have to wait many years later to discover many other sports which he never had the opportunity or time to explore, and where he was to show much promise.

His height now lent itself to increased speed covering the ground much more readily on a hockey pitch than previously. This prompted a move from full back – a relatively 'safe' position to introduce a newcomer to the game, except when having to stand on the goal line to defend or deflect shots aimed directly at him – to a midfield role where racing from the top of one D to the other was the order of the day, covering maybe 80% of the pitch.

It also had its disadvantages. The lower half of the bunk bed he had occupied for the last eighteen years was stretched to its limits. Comfort was only to be had by sleeping diagonally, preferably with his head away from the wall, where patches of condensation regularly grouped together to discolour what had always been described by his parents to others as sunshine yellow.

In fact in earlier times he had been fascinated by the darker blotches of wall, some of which bore a remarkable resemblance to countries he had come across in geography. There was a very good image of the UK, another larger one resembling Australia and a more indistinct one, which could have been one of two or three countries, depending on the angle you looked at it.

Decades later when he had to clear out that same room, he reflected on how dismal it all looked. Run down and damp with that solitary, brown, cylindrical electric heater, which ran the length of the bed, but was hardly ever used to save electricity. His father had later sequestered the room as a storage place for unopened Christmas presents – usually tools of some description with endless uses proposed on the packaging – none of which were either practical or met his needs. And then there were his wine jars: tens of five litre demijohns, some still with their airlocks in, others with bungs. The contents varied in colour from a pale citrus yellow assumed to be pear wine, to a deeper yellow-brown liquid most likely to be apple wine, to a richer dark crimson concoction, which suspiciously looked like the lethal sloe wine.

A glance through the aged lace curtain behind him saw the vine overgrowing from the front door, smothering the light from the three sections of window but the rays were strong. Just as he had remembered them while working at his small, two foot square desk, now submerged beneath split and yellowing cardboard boxes, filled to the brim with clutter. How dismal too, old age must have been for him.

The strengthening sun recalled working like stink for his A Levels in the hottest summer of all time, while nursing a broken ankle – or rather a break just above it – from a foolish, impromptu cricket practice in the nets while wearing sandals. 'How stupid of me!' he thought, a horrendous mistake which resulted in him watching all his peers rejoice at the end of exams by spending hours in the public swimming pool, the only place to cool off and sit on the grass afterwards on their towels, discussing nothing in particular.

His earliest memories returned apace, between the ages of five and seven years, when he had spent many waking and sleeping hours watching the dim but warm candle light of a coal tar lamp, inhaling its life-giving odour to recover from a series of childhood illnesses, including bronchitis. Doctor Gordon was a frequent visitor to his bedroom, largely with curtains closed, his grey pinstripe suit cutting a dark silhouette against a winter sun trying to break through. His mother had always seemed melodramatic in referring to that time as "the time we nearly lost you". She was not given to melodrama though. Her constant presence saw him through those tough days. Her patience and resilience were well known, but her parenting skill was tested to the absolute limit one morning.

George had awoken to a strange warmth against his lower right leg underneath his pyjama trouser. In stirring from a deep sleep, his unconscious mulled over the possibilities for its cause. Was it a relic of a dream, but he had no waking recollection of being next to a fire or an oven?

Was it the leftovers of a wet dream, in which case he would need to rush to the toilet to avoid embarrassment, hoping not to encounter his mother or sister on the way?

What a shock that was the very first time it happened. He had heard talk at the senior school of wet dreams with no explanation of what these were, but that talk had subsided many years before. Relatively late into his teens, he had awoken from an unusual dream which seemed real enough, walking along one of the main streets of the town. There were many people passing him, mostly children with their mothers and some other women shopping. As each one passed him by in the dream, he found himself avoiding eye contact by looking down below their chin line. To his amazement he didn't realise how different each woman's breasts were. Guess he'd never noticed them before, but now they were making him hot and restless. Something happened in his bed to wake him up and he looked down to discover an unknown pasty liquid, besmirched on the inside of his pyjama trousers. He had stepped down sheepishly from the bottom bunk and moved silently to the bathroom to clean up and hoped no one noticed. Above all the unexpected nature of things, it annoyed him intensely – 'Why doesn't anyone tell you about this shit?' he blurted out to no one in particular on a dog walk.

He recognised therefore that this was not the same warmth, as it did not go cold and wet soon after.

Before he could arrive at a satisfactory explanation, the warm patch moved. Even more disconcerting, it was moving up his trouser leg beyond his knee. This was a complete shock that a living creature had managed to enter his bed, when he religiously tucked in his sheets and blankets on all sides before going to bed each night.

He retracted his leg at speed. The warm patch disappeared, thank goodness. He hastily jumped out of bed, put on his slippers and threw the bed clothes back up to contain whatever it was. Relating the incident to his mum, she leapt into action and grabbed the aluminium tool used to empty the fire ash tray and strode purposefully into his bedroom.

Bending under the top bunk to get a closer look, she inched the bed sheets back towards the bottom, searching both sides as she went, but was forced to declare once she'd reached the bottom, 'There's nothing there.'

'How can that be?' he protested, 'I didn't dream this up. There's something moving around in my bed and if we can't find it, then I'm sleeping in the main room tonight!'

'Alright, let's look a bit more.' she acquiesced, hoping that it wasn't a wild goose chase, except that would have been easier to spot. 'Aha,' she exclaimed, 'There you have it, tucked right down into the very corner of the sheets.' She began poking the tool forcefully down into that space. 'You were right George, here's your intruder.' She withdrew from underneath the bunk holding a stunned mouse by its tail. 'Must have come in with those potatoes you both brought in last week.'

With the disaster of having to sleep on the front room floor averted – and jolly cold that could be once the fire went out – he returned to the scullery to make his breakfast and thanked his mum profusely for coming to his rescue, as she did so often.

She had been an amazingly resolute, brave and forthright mother to him. The edges of his lips turned upwards as he recalled her trick among the primary school boys, who were testing her a little one break time. She had been employed in George's last years at the school as a canteen assistant. He was never sure if that was a conscious move to be closer to him and keep a watchful eye on him or whether it was a fortuitous coincidence. It was comforting to see a friendly-but-no-favours face during the day, matched only by the presence of the famous Auntie Ada. She made it her business to look out for those children who hated cauliflower, George among them, to spirit the offending vegetable away while the teacher on duty was not looking. 'Eat every last bit of it!' often was the cry echoing from the end of the dining room, which also doubled up as the gym.

'Don't you worry,' came the comforting whisper in his ear, 'you can get down and go out to play... now that it's gone.' Didn't they just love Auntie Ada!

Back out on the field, some older boys were surrounding his mother in the shade on an old elm tree. At the base were some tall, overgrown nettles which all the boys were very wary of.

'No need to be scared of nettles!' enticed his mother in her unofficial capacity as part-time illusionist. With those words, she plucked a long nettle up by its roots, turned it facing downwards to the ground and ran her hand effortlessly from top to bottom without stopping, wincing and, remarkably for him too, without being stung multiple times over.

'How'd you do that?' the group echoed in unison.

'Simple,' she said, 'look at the underside of each leaf and notice how all the shards under the leaves point downwards. So long as you follow the direction of the shards, they cannot harm you.'

No one ever felt the same intimidation or antagonism towards nettles again after that, resulting in instant recognition among his peers, which made George immensely proud of the nettle tamer.

For now though, all he knew was that the practice of sealing himself into his bed especially at the bottom end was no longer practical as it cramped his toes.

He had not given much thought as to the speed of his own development compared with the rest of his school friends. He was just glad to have caught up with them and understood what his schoolmates had been on about for years.

His musical preferences – or maybe it was just his ears developing – were also changing. From his parents' small selection of records and their radio listening habits, he became more aware of the power of music.

Sundays were always an enjoyable day of the week. Listening to the radio where 'Round the Horne', 'The Clitheroe Kid' and the 'Navy Lark' took turns to keep the whole family entertained and allowed their lunch to go down. Laughter and a limited amount of 78s playing music on the Dansette record player were as staple as any of the other food presented to them at mealtimes. It was one such LP of Miki and Griff which had introduced George to the exquisite sound of harmonisation between two voices in a delicious duet.

Third Encounter

With his parent's blessing, he had joined the local church choir at St. Mary's as a treble and continued to attend matins and evensong for many years. His voice transitioned to the alto register until a very late teenage year, before moving on to tenor at seventeen and eventually, at nineteen, to a bass voice without interruption.

Punctuality was not always his best suit. On occasions he would arrive breathless, having run the last hundred yards through the cemetery, robing up in double quick time – his gym teacher would have been so proud!

For the majority of the time, entering the church via the vestry door instilled a level of calm and peace, which his increasingly complex world could not give. The thick flint walls standing firm on the chalky landscape, as they had done since the 12th century, absorbed the sun's warmth through its immense rectangular windows to comfort and give company to those within.

How strange but wonderful it was to think that it was at that very font that he had been baptised… not that he remembered that occasion. In the same way he came to appreciate how special his home village was: a house where he had been born in the upper bedroom and raised there for the whole of his young life. Bumping into the district nurse around the village – the very nurse who had delivered him – was always a pleasure. Nurse Unwin lived next to the police house. Not a location he cycled by much, as it was on one of the three intersecting roads which defined the triangular shaped village. He tended to keep to the inside of that triangle where there was less traffic. There it boasted more common land, like The Bailey, to explore and play games in. She always had a generous word and expressed surprise at his growth latterly too, as she craned her neck up towards him, to look him in the eye. He felt they were all family in that community.

The church choir too became another family to belong to. For the best part of eleven years, the same people came together on Friday evenings to rehearse the music for the following weekend services. Tuesdays were – and probably still are – the bell ringers night. George learnt one of his first big words there at the age of nine: a campanologist. That only because two of their number rang bells as well as sang in the choir. They were Laurie, an accomplished and long-time tenor mainstay, and the choirmaster who insisted on being called Bertie. As a nine year old, this freedom reminded him of the one afforded to him by his Grandad, a freedom he was told came to him at quite an early age. While he was still only four years of age, his nan would recount how this young boy would scamper round her house looking for her sister, shouting at the top of his voice 'Dawn! Where are you, Dawn?'

'That is Great Aunt Dawn to you, little fella.' she would try to impress on him, but George would have none of it. The two of them, Dawn and George that is, remained the best of friends. In spite of the distance involved, because Dawn had left for Canada shortly after the war ended with her new husband, she made frequent trips back to England and made sure to tell him of her travel stories each time.

George was made to feel right at home in the choir from the start. He was introduced to Pam and Ella, the soprano and alto voices respectively. They stood out for him because of their contrasting hair colour, both beyond shoulder length, the former blonde, the latter pure black. When dressed in their surplice gowns at services, this difference was even more striking. George was to support Pam at first with his treble voice and was lucky enough to sit next to Ella when his voice began its inexorable slide down the register. He remained an alto with her for more than three years, even retaining that register as a countertenor, once the move to tenor was in train.

By then, some new houses had swept away all but the farmhouse of a neighbouring farm on the High Street and replaced it with overspill units 'easy and quick to build;' he thought, 'pretty ugly to look at!' as if having an opinion on such things was a natural part of his growth curve. Not long after, Pam and Ella left the village to go onto pastures new and they were replaced, in number anyway, by a Ricky and a Joan as tenor and soprano.

It was good to see some of the newcomers to the village becoming involved. Jonny, another bass, also joined swelling the choir numbers to a ten year high. So many of the existing villagers, centred around the five main farming families originally, were disconcerted by the development, thinking it would turn into a dormitory village. Well, on this showing alone, they appeared to have overstated that. These new people were exceedingly friendly and wanted to make a positive contribution. They all became firm friends of an ever expanding family.

On their way back they took the same short route, often stopping off at the mobile fish and chip trailer which parked on the spare space next to The Lamb, one of four local pubs. Fish on Friday was almost a religion in itself. Once their fish in newspaper had been bought, they would talk about current affairs and of local village topics for the last shared two hundred yards on the way home. On the nights that fish was not taken, the walks were protracted over a longer period to talk more. As time progressed, George realised how stimulating adult conversation can be. He grew to prefer it and as his university years beckoned, he sought advice from the one person, Joan, who had not long since finished her own course to take up a position in an adult learning centre-cum-alternative sixth form college.

'Joan was different to the other two men.' George observed a little obviously. Jonny and Ricky seemed set already into a married life, giving voice to ecstasy, frustration and complaints in equal measure. 'Old before their time.' he thought, recalling how he himself had been dubbed as having a 'wise head on young shoulders' on more than one occasion. This notion was entirely lost on him during and even now at the end of these teenage years. It seemed superfluous to everyday living, as far as he could see. It was just another thing which went over the head of those young shoulders, as an irrelevance and of little or no practical use or consequence.

'No home to go to?' jibed Jonny one evening as they overtook George and Joan, who were deep in conversation with each other. Raising an acknowledging arm in their direction and with a polite laugh, they returned to their discussion.

Clearly young at heart, Joan seemed to understand George's situation so much better than anyone else. Her softly lilting Edinburgh tone was soothing to his ears, while she was expounding a particularly long theory of the effects of reaching junctures in one's life.

Voices were important, he realised more and more. None more so than one voice in harmony with another. Another soprano had joined the choir called Toni, short for Antonia he surmised, but never knew and never dared to ask. Another lady in her early to mid-thirties, with strikingly golden-brown hair curved slightly upwards as it took residence on her shoulders. She and Joan got on very well together. Her voice seemed to be from one of the home counties, was educated and her syntax clear; when singing its crystal tones soared high up the scales with ease and was a pure delight to listen to. Enamoured of how she came to perfect such a sound, her generosity overwhelmed George when she spoke about George's own beautiful voice to Bertie, the choirmaster, and how she would very much like to sing a duet at the earliest opportunity with him.

George had been used to being called on to sing solos in hymns, anthems or Christmas choir specials from either of the two orange or green carol books most choirs seemed to sing from. But this was something entirely different. They stayed behind after the main choir had dispersed: a demanding piece had been selected to showcase both their voices blending together as one in some sections and in perfect counterpoint in others. He felt very privileged, not only to blend voices with an amazing soprano, but also just to be in her presence. She had a certain aura about her. It hadn't escaped his notice on her arrival how all the male voices surrounded her like bees to the proverbial honeypot, so taken were they with her petite beauty as they saw it, no doubt. For that reason, he had distanced himself from the throng, feeling that there was perhaps too much attention being given to the new arrival and not enough recognition to the existing female voices. So, while being chosen to sing with Toni on this one piece, he was sensitive to Joan's feelings and spent more time speaking with her on their way back from practices, once normal service had been resumed and the event passed.

Joan was nearer to his height, as he had now reached six feet one at the age of nineteen. She was perhaps five feet ten or so. He could only guess at it really. Others had trekked off to university that year, but his enforced choice was to defer a year, which gave him the chance to earn some much needed money and expanded his conversation to a working life. 'So much to tell you...' he would begin as he regaled her with his stories and incidents, which made both of them crease up with laughter or laugh out loud. They would glance about them cautiously, hoping neighbours in the vicinity had not been disturbed.

Work Experience

He only took one job during that year out. Not the most romantic, attractive-sounding or career-propelling job: a petrol pump assistant, working for a man with a moustache, well on the way to being a handlebar variety, to rival that of the great Jimmy Edwards.

Luckily he only encountered the owner once before being given the job, twice during the course of it to speak of, and once at the end... when George was fired!

Thereby hangs a tale. Apart from giving his unfortunate name to the business, the owner Mr Willey spent all his time in the centre of town showroom, selling cars in his grey pinstripe. The working garage end of the business, where George was to work on the forecourt, doubled up as an open air car sales plot as well as having garage repairs taken care of out the back. Mr Willey's only excursion to the working end was to dip his fingers into the till, extract wads of cash from it and scribble a hasty note, which he inserted under the £20 note clasp. George had noticed that the site manager had always dropped everything on his approach, which he put down to deference to the owner to do whatever he commanded. He only learnt later of the real purpose.

NIPPER

Not that much later indeed, because after an initial three weeks of working alongside his two co-workers – Lee, the site manager and Ches, the very entertaining, real world kind of guy, Romanian by birth and British by ingrained cynicism – Lee announced to them both 'Right. I'm off.' That was no surprise as five o'clock had already arrived and George was already preparing to mount his trusty steed to cycle the five miles back home.

'See you tomorrow', George called out as he pushed off.

'No, wait,' he said, 'what I mean is I haven't had a holiday for the past two years and you are perfectly capable of managing on your own. The last three weeks have proved that to me.'

It was on the tip of George's tongue to say 'Flattery will get you nowhere. Get away with you', when it dawned on him how his manager's hunched stance adopted over the last weeks were just a façade for an oppressed, deeply-held conviction that he had been wronged by his employer. George agreed without a moment's hesitation. He could see immediately how Lee was now standing up straighter, the weight lifted partially from his shoulders and his small but stocky frame had a purposeful step about it now. George also wondered if he would also stop the disgusting habit of taking snuff and blowing his nose into the same brown stained handkerchief during these last weeks, which placed him firmly in a different century. Perhaps that too was symptomatic of the same underlying cause.

Lee lost no time in briefing George on the necessary tasks to become Site Manager for the next three weeks. Principal among which were two specific ones: first he had to take the till roll home with him every night to carry out the reconciliation with moneys taken. Second and more importantly he stressed, was the monitoring of the guv'nor.

"E weren't too good at Maths, which is why 'e went straight into selling cars!' he confided in George, continuing 'which is why, when 'e comes snooping into the till, you watch 'im like an 'awk'.

'But it is his business. He can take money out whenever he likes, I suppose', George surmised naively.

'No. You don't get it.' came the reply, 'You count how much 'e takes out by looking over his shoulder, because as sure as eggs are eggs, 'e'll write down the wrong number on the note ... that is, if you can even read the note.'

'Do this and you have a good chance of reconciliation.' Duly noted and he wasn't wrong either. First till raid was £20 short on the note and subsequent raids out by between ten and thirty pounds.

With Lee back in the saddle after his well-earned rest, all seemed brighter now with him. Jovial to a turn, his endlessly complaining, angular face now gave way to a much more pleasant countenance. His mood lightened with our regulars, who extended some much needed perks in our direction. Ches would poke his head round the door of the tiny area where the till was, which barely could hold two of them in it. Ches, the slimmer of the two, was accommodated quite easily, but Lee posed an obstacle too great to circumvent once in there.

'Did you see that lady in the herald, just now?' Ches panted with anticipation, having taken another break from the routine garage repair work that filled his days.

'I would do anything for her. I mean anything.'

So much was his admiration that he pushed past Lee and myself to exit via the shopfront door, to engage her as she went to get back into her car. The shop door closed quickly behind him, as designed, and neither of them could hear their conversation. George noticed she smiled at one point.

'Do you think he just repeated what he said to us just now?' enquired George in utter disbelief.

'Wouldn't put it past 'im', replied Lee, 'That'll be the Romanian blood in 'im, I expect.'

George stood back, seeing to the next customer who had entered the shop, but couldn't help wondering how far men would go to get noticed by the opposite sex. Another steep learning curve, he thought.

So things seemed to be going swimmingly until one lunchtime, when both the other two had gone to lunch. A customer needed his oil checked and when advised it was too low, asked for it to be topped up for him. George obliged in this pre-self-service world: releasing the bonnet catch, lifting the bonnet, undoing the filler cap and placing it on the side, while he discharged a quart of oil into the engine.

Replacing the bonnet, the man left in his Volvo. Barely had George re-entered the shop, when the same man returned shortly afterwards, as luck would have it, just before the paunched and suited garage owner pulled onto the forecourt to fill up.

'What's the meaning of this?' the man screamed at George, whose armpits resorted to that awkward feeling of being separated from his body at an impending confrontation with a raised voice of one much older than him. 'Why do my underarms always get so nervous like that? Will I never be rid of this feeling?' he muttered to himself, annoyed but having to suppress everything in front of the customer. He kept his cool, despatched himself quickly out the door with a rag and cleaning materials.

'I'm going to lunch now. It had better be clean by the time I get back!' the man said at the top of his voice, turning the head of the garage owner. Managing somehow not to blush with embarrassment, he had to explain the circumstances to the owner, whose face turned the corners of his moustache downwards in an unforgiving frown. Given his success with till reconciliation over the past three weeks, George thought it would stand him in better stead than he would have been otherwise and hoped the owner would overlook this, his first blunder. That misapprehension did not last more than a week, when another much bigger calamity awaited them both and was the reason for the second meeting with the owner.

That would be the not insignificant matter of the new Chrysler. Joan couldn't wait to hear more and looked forward with anticipation to their meeting up again after choir practice the following week. George continued as if they had never separated from the week before ...

On a sharp, crispy morning in early March, George's day began the same as it usually did. The pleasant five mile ride into work, opening up with Lee, taking the meter readings on each pump and starting every vehicle angled at 45° to the forecourt, designed to entice what the owner would call 'passing trade'. In fact plenty of cars passed by every day and not a single second hand car ever sold the entire time he was there!

The cars had to be started and moved backwards and forwards into their familiar slot, the familiarity stamped into the grass verge, where each car's heavy shadow ensured no grass ever saw the light of day beneath it. The surface was a drab brown collaboration of flattened mud, wasted former shoots, shrivelled and twisted, like old straw with an occasional worm rising to the surface at the vibrations caused by the moving tyres. On the odd occasion a blackbird, ever the opportunist, would descend upon the revealed bare lot with breakneck speed, draw its prey out of the ground after a short struggle and disappear off across the busy road, diving into the nearest safe bush haven.

The reason for these seemingly pointless manoeuvres was to free off the hand brakes, which regularly fused themselves rigid on frosty nights and would protect the ephemeral potential customer from the unnerving experience of trying to reverse out of the space without success and stalling the car. George made a mental note never to buy a car from there, ever.

Shortly after 8.30am George's attention was drawn to a shiny new registration plate, which pulled onto the forecourt to fill up. He instantly recognised the model from a conversation with Ches earlier in the week. On that occasion, again early in the morning, he had been invited excitedly out back to witness a rare sight. That of a brand new Chrysler with a scorch mark in the centre of the bonnet, the size of a football, burned back to the bare metal. Ches enjoyed recounting how he had been called out the night before to a fire incident to recover this car, only to find its carburettor had a malfunction, which set light to the bonnet from beneath.

'Wow, that's amazing!' said George, stupefied at the concentrated destruction of some poor soul's pride and joy.

WORK EXPERIENCE

With his hand on the petrol pump nozzle, George inserted it into the fuel tank, lifting from its deepest insertion back a few centimetres to avoid the potential blowback and resultant dousing of his trousers in petrol: a lesson he'd learnt early on at the garage, when an entire day had been spent stinking of fuel.

'How's it going with the new motor?' George asked to make polite conversation. 'Great', came the reply from a man in his late forties, maybe early fifties.

'Hasn't caught fire yet then?' this question more than bemusing a suddenly, much more engaged customer. 'Well, no.' the man replied, with eyebrows raised curiously to one side.

The summary was kept brief as his tank was almost full. He paid in cash and drove away, cautiously it might be said.

'Phone for you, Georgie', cried out Lee from the shop door. How he hated being called that. He was sure he did it on purpose, but no matter. A call at work was indeed a rarity. His ears were pinned back as he put the receiver to his ear and found it was the garage owner on the other end.

'Who's been blabbing about Chrysler fires on the forecourt just now?' George sunk onto a chair and was about to explain 'I was just chatting ...' when he was cut short.

'That customer you just "chatted to" was a fleet manager and had just bought two Chryslers. He's now cancelled orders for four more based on your testimony!'

'I suggest in future you keep your mouth firmly shut when on the forecourt', he continued to ram the point home with justifiable annoyance. George prepared himself for the worst thinking this may be his last day of employment, but to his utter amazement, the owner replaced the handset and no more was said on the matter. He was extremely grateful for this and from a start of rock bottom, his opinion of the owner began to change.

Nothing much changed over the following months, ten in total, when he learnt that his nan had passed away. Though nowhere near as close to her as he had been to her husband, his grandad, he was saddened at the thought of that generation chapter coming to a close.

While his early memories of her stern disposition were not the happiest, he had come to like her as he grew older. She had waited until quite late in his teens to ask if he could run a couple of errands down to the shop for her on a Saturday morning. The few items she listed each week were no chore to carry on his bike. The house was empty now, with all of her progeny having flown the coop, emigrated to Australia or New Zealand or passed away in Sammie's case. The house smelled damp and her position didn't much change from one Saturday to another. He could not tell if this was a conscious decision not to heat the house, determined as she undoubtedly was, or whether she had fallen on hard times. Anyway, he obliged her every week and continued to do so, even when he had arrived earlier than normal on one occasion, to find another young lad crossing him on his bike on the path leading up the front garden. George put two and two together and confirmed with the lad that he had indeed been doing a spot of shopping for the old lady for quite some time.

So it was the company he presumed she wanted, not that he considered himself any catch in that department, as his conversation was limited to family, his job and the weather. Current affairs only made an entrance into his life with the

WORK EXPERIENCE

advent eventually of a wooden boxed television, a hand-me-down to his family it seemed from its battered edges and faded surround. It took pride of place beneath the window sill, pushing the Singer sewing machine in its beautiful, gleaming mahogany cabinet to the right. George's small transistor radio was allowed to sit on top of this cabinet next to the Dansette record player, which fell more and more into disuse. No one in his house was allowed to watch the commercial channel, but the main public broadcast channel was and, once a second public channel arrived, George understood the meaning of 625 lines across a screen, which gave a much better picture quality.

From that chance meeting, George was relieved of his local grandson duty, so that his Saturdays were now his own. But he was still sad: not just for his mum, who surely missed her though could only tolerate her in small doses, but also for her sister in Canada and George's personal matriarchal favourite, his Great Aunt Dawn.

It didn't take him long to reach out to her daughter, his Aunt Carrie-Anne, to arrive at dates for a three week stay. This would include spending half the time in Vancouver where Dawn was and half the time on the Island bearing the same name, where Carrie-Anne and her son Chad lived. He'd seen photos of the house enclosed in Christmas cards from her, which were so captivating: built to her and her husband's design, a double-A roofed house and studio, where she would have young budding artists to stay on the banks of a perhaps 20 metre wide, fast-flowing, spectacularly clean river with a wilderness beyond: endless inspiration in shedloads.

Joan was happy for George that he was taking a well-earned break, before going up to university in September and spoke freely, saying 'Roll on the day when you return and can tell me all about your adventure.'

An adventure it certainly was. Even before the flight was due, a last minute change meant the lower cost airline could no longer offer him that flight. They were extremely apologetic in a letter to him, offering him instead a flight on the same day, with a better airline and asking if he wouldn't mind extending his stay to five weeks. 'Would I mind?' he cried out loud incredulously in his bedroom the day before he was due to leave. 'Just try and stop me!' he exclaimed emphatically. He hurried to tell the news to his mum, before eagerly running back to his room to pack. No time to lose.

The flight was deliciously luxurious for him, as it was his first time in the air. 'I could get used to this', he thought while savouring the extras on board. On a flight with relatively few passengers, he enjoyed chatting with the hostesses, who were exceedingly kind to his British accent which they seemed to enjoy, though he couldn't say why.

The highlights while there in Vancouver were dining out, savouring the delights of the quarry garden at Queen Elizabeth Park and being taught how to use chopsticks for the first time. 'We'll be going to a real Chinese restaurant,' Dawn insisted, 'not one of those takeaways you have so many of in England.' He was none the wiser, having barely heard of that phenomenon, let alone being able to afford it. Other treats were travelling up the Okanagan valley with its row upon row of apple trees of every description, a virgin forest of giant redwoods and a failed attempt to travel into the US without a visa. His hosts must not have known it as they pulled up at the customs post. They had prepared George with the phrase that was always asked first upon arrival. 'Where have you just come from?' – A simple enough question to which I was told that 'Vancouver' was an adequate answer. However, a brief look at my passport revealed no valid visa and we were turned around, driving the short semi-circular route to the other customs post for traffic going in the opposite direction.

When asked the exact same question first, George piped up from the back seat of the ageing but stately Buick 'From that customs post over there', pointing in its direction. Smiles all around, including from the border guard left them all with a pleasant taste after what could have proved to be a fruitless journey. The Okanagan made that impossible of course. Samples were duly gleaned and devoured before the car journey concluded.

The stay on Vancouver Island was equally impressive, if not more so, due to the completely untamed nature which lay around every bend. The arrival was distinctly inauspicious however, when an untamed gander pinned him behind his two suitcases at the front door for what seemed to be forever, while his Aunt foraged for the key round the back: his worst nightmare. Thank goodness he had packed two bags for the extended stay and not one. Otherwise, the gander would have had a clear view of his ankles and head stooped, would have stopped at nothing until it had found bare flesh to grab at.

He had known this terrifying feeling once, and only once before, in his grandfather's (on his father's side) orchard where, as an impressionable seven or eight year old, he had been sent into an unkempt part of the orchard. There, ageing fruit trees – mostly pear and apples with an exceptional greengage tree – maintained their height above the dried grass and weeds that stood higher than him and from which the winged menace appeared, heading straight for him. 'Why me, for goodness' sake?' he pleaded, but his supplication was not heard.

It pecked at his soft flesh on the still chubby legs protruding from the old shorts he was wont to wear. He darted off towards the gate, screaming and shouting at the top of his voice till he reached safety. Only then did the sobs subside enough for him to hear anyone else.

'They don't hurt. Just ignore them' announced the more senior among them, followed with a 'Don't let them get the better of you, for goodness' sake' from his son. Distancing himself from them both was the only way he could console himself. For his father that lasted just for the day but for his grandfather, it was another nail in his coffin.

The moment at Carrie-Anne's front door passed with the opening of the solid wooden door. He was greeted by the relative comfort of an open space with strong beams supporting the upper studio floor, where all conversation could be unintentionally overheard: a threatening atmosphere for some, but a blessed freedom to roam without doors closing off areas intended for adults only. The overriding feeling in this rural Canadian idyll was one of a warm welcome.

Rising out of his rocking chair, the Texan frame strode towards him and grasped him firmly, if a little too firmly, by the hand crushing the very life out of several of his fingers. This was Bob. A towering presence when stood tall, but also a gentle giant when reclining back into his rocking chair and taking up the rhythmical turning of a jam jar he held in both hands. 'What is that?' asked George. 'Why, I'm making butter.'

WORK EXPERIENCE

said Bob prosaically, as an accomplished regular activity it was his duty and wish to perform.

Fascinating it was to hear how a young calf is dependent on those first few drafts of milk from its mother to impart all manner of antibodies, nutrients and other elements which were amazing for a calf, but which made lousy milk and butter for humans. George could feel himself wishing how he would have loved Bob to have been his Biology teacher!

In a matter of a few minutes and after one particular turn of the jar, the hitherto liquid stopped sloshing about and became an instant, solid, yellow cylindrical mass of pure butter. The sight of that experience never left him.

Joan's jaw visibly dropped at this point, as she too had never been brought up on a farm, in fact not been within 50 miles of one. At least George had his harvest time experience to fall back on, as well as the testimony of a distant uncle, who had remarkably wide fingers when he came to tea once. George had been mesmerised by these inflated, rubber glove hands. It turned out he was a farmer of a dairy herd and gave George a quick lesson on how to milk a cow, should the need ever arise.

The stay on Vancouver Island culminated in a three day trip into the interior with Chad and Jed, a friend from nearby. As they pushed off in a 14 foot 'ali' – aluminium boat that had a single, small outboard motor on the back – Chad announced to George 'Well, say goodbye to civilisation. That's back there on the jetty where my mum left us. Ahead is nothing but wilderness!'

He wasn't wrong and it did not disappoint. Deadheads to avoid in the water: they were long-fallen remnants of trees, whose legacy was a visible protrusion from the lake's surface or a concealed stub beneath the surface, which could leave a gash in the underside and mean the premature end to the trip. George was placed as lookout to good effect; once on dry land, there were ribbon trails to follow, views to take in and Jed insisting he'd come across bear dung; stream and small river crossings with full backpacks challenged their sense of balance. The further they climbed George noticed, the narrower the tree trunks felled as river crossings became, the faster the water flowed and gushed, until the tree crossing consisted of not one but two saplings. George would not have bothered cutting them down for the local bonfire, so tiny were they, and yet here they were, doing a fine balancing act so as not to end up in the water.

On one such crossing, George joined in with Chad on saying a cheery and loud 'Hello campers!' upstream to a shape spotted traversing the stream above them. No sooner had the words left their lips, than they both gasped and a concerned, hirsute face glanced in their direction for a lifetime, before continuing to cross over to the other side. That was to be George's first and only encounter with a brown bear.

A breathtaking waterfall awaited them at the conclusion of the trail, but not before another smaller waterfall ran into a deep substantial crater in the side of the mountain. Its name, which George could not determine whether it was just a coincidence or a joke at his expense, was Englishman's Falls.

'Lucky you packed your trunks,' jibed Chad, 'it's said that it's soooo cold that only an Englishman can stand to get in!'

'How about it? George sounds very English to me!' goaded Jed to force the issue. Reluctant to disavow his hosts of any such tale as either myth or legend, he did what he considered to be his English duty, to hold up his end for Queen and country, and in he went. 'Crikey, that's cold. No not cold, freezing', he thought but uttered instead, 'Come on in, the water's lovely.' He was not taken up on his offer and the legend was reinforced.

His adventure came to a close too early of course and the airport beckoned. Memories aplenty, photos to develop and renewal of a long-standing friendship with his closest matriarch as well as a newly found camaraderie with a Canadian cousin, made the journey all the more sweet.

On returning to the UK five weeks later, he made the five mile journey into work but did not need to dismount from his bike since he was greeted by the garage owner. Oddly and completely unexpectedly, he was helping out in the shop, greeting George with 'You don't expect to still have a job, do you?' George realised the question was largely rhetorical, instead opting for the briefest of responses, 'No. I suppose not.' He took his leave of the site and the two firm friends he had made, bidding farewell to Ches and Lee with the broadest of smiles.

'See you around guys. It's been great working alongside you. Thank you for everything. Take care.'

With that he cycled back, his heart as light as it had been on the way in, half knowing that he would be in the brown and smellies, but with the other half not caring to continue working for such an unprepossessing owner. Besides, he was off to university soon and had just spent the most marvellous last few weeks in a country of opportunities and experiences he could never have imagined. The travel bug was now well and truly in his veins.

Everything in Moderation

Being a little out of routine and with no work now left George with some much appreciated downtime. Not the kind that slept in till midday, although advantage was taken under the banner of rest and recuperation, which he felt he had earnt. There was still much to prepare for however, and with the lightest evenings still very much on offer, he enjoyed the long days catching up with tasks which had eluded him.

With no other transport available, he took long walks around his familiar village, remembering instances of exhilaration, fear, uncertainty and unadulterated happiness.

Walking towards Tower Hill he recalled hours spent outside a newcomer's house, along with two other boys, all vying for the attentions of the new girl in the village – the stunning Lesley with shoulder length dark hair, well-built frame and generous proportions with it. Turning down towards Pollard's Way, he traversed the regular bitumen lines across the road, which used to double up as half-tennis courts, at a time when traffic was unheard of during the day. He wondered where his long-time friend Andrew was now. His house was perched on the corner of a line of young elm trees, so close together that it made good sport to time each other going from one end to the other – only a matter of 70 metres or so – without touching the ground.

Closer to home, turning down Little Lane, he looked nervously and instinctively behind him to see if he was being followed. The same fear sent spasms through his armpit once more.

The lane had grown somewhat smaller now and not through overgrowing hedgerows, but the width seemed unrecognisably diminished. Glancing to his left he espied the neat rows of vegetables cultivated by a local market gardener. He had turned to growing cabbages mostly now, perhaps due to the losses he had suffered to his carrots over a number of earlier years, when young boys' appetites had to be satisfied. Far easier than scrumping apples, which meant reaching or climbing up into the branches in plain sight. Crawling like commandos between the rows was much more fun and there was nothing like the scent of a freshly plucked carrot.

He hadn't long been back inside when there came a knock at the back door, which was always left open. 'Come in', George said cheerfully glad to have a visitor in the middle of the day. To his surprise it was Joan's figure which filled the daylight space, her face drawn and pale, breaking into sobs as she stepped down into the living room.

'Whatever is the matter?' asked George, 'Let me go and make you a cup of tea.' He had heard or read somewhere recently that warming up from the inside is what people in distress need. The thought of ginger wine and its famously green labelled bottle came into his mind as something that might have done the job too, but thought twice about offering alcohol as a young adult to an older one. Ginger wine was his own first ever drop of alcohol that he had tasted at a tender age many years before. That not only warmed him up inside, but sent him snuggling down onto the small, semi-circular carpet in front of the television, where he gladly cuddled up to his dog and went to bed much later than normal as a result. However, given the time of day it was not appropriate, so tea it was.

His offer was taken up and he wasted no time in boiling the water and making a robust cup of tea. His mum after all – it was no secret within the family – had won a prize for her tea making: a delightful print of Salisbury Cathedral on a summer's afternoon, bathed in sunlight not unlike that of this fateful afternoon.

Once Joan had settled herself into a chair and sipped her tea thoughtfully, she recounted the awful events of the last ten minutes which changed her life. She had been walking her dog in the Bailey late that morning, when she came across something strange a way off. In the distance, quite close to the path, there appeared to be a dark pile of cloth or belongings. Her mind considered someone perhaps carelessly allowing heaped clothes to fall from a pram, while pushing it over the rough terrain, but the more she thought about it, the more reasonable explanations eluded her.

It was only on closer inspection as she neared the large object that it dawned on her that this was a man lying still on the grass, not moving a muscle. Fear gripped her very soul. Anna from a nearby cottage just outside the Bailey gate happened on the same spot about the same time, when she heard Joan's cries. Anna dashed back into the house to raise the alarm and call the police, who were there after only a few minutes. The man was pronounced dead at the scene by an ambulance crew. After taking a short statement, Joan was allowed to leave, her body still shaking from the sight of that poor man, shaking now as she retold the incident next to him.

Her hand gripped his forearm tightly. 'I've never seen a dead body before and hope never to see one again.' she said, closing her eyes in silent prayer. George had no words, just rose with her as she stood up out of the chair. The fire was out and George wished it had not been. She needed warmth.

'I was so frightened George,' she confided softly, 'so frightened.' Her use of his name touched him. He didn't know quite why, but he was physically and visibly moved by her terrible ordeal. 'So frightened', she repeated, at once putting her arms round his neck and drawing him to her. He responded with like, gazing over her shoulder at the dead embers of the fire against the dark lumps of coal, a futile effort to revive something which had no life left in it. A tear rolled out of his eye and he too felt the need for warmth, hugging her more closely than before.

'I'm sorry to be a nuisance', she excused herself unnecessarily. 'Not at all,' he comforted as they stood apart, 'you are always welcome. The door is always open.' He fumbled for words to soothe her recovery and prepare her for the outside world again. She took her leave and George watched her invisibly through the net curtain at the front window. As she turned to close the green gate, before stepping down onto the path, her head remained bowed. He watched as she made her way past the Dorothy Perkins pink rambling roses along the front hedge and wondered if he should pick her some of those fragrant blooms to cheer her up, but thought it not the right moment.

It was but a few days later that they bumped into each other at their Friday talking spot, opposite where the old butcher's shop had been on the corner of her road. The change was palpable, their friendship deepened and their eyes made more contact than before. He could see her latent pain at the incident and the need for reassurance.

'You'll be heading off to university soon. My husband has given me permission to take you out for a drink to send you off. Can you believe that?'

This was quite unexpected, but kind, given her recent experience, all too vivid in both their minds. 'Sure,' he said, 'I look forward to it.' Plans were made as to location and time, before she turned to go. For the first time George noticed how her tight jumper accentuated her ample breasts and how her bottom protruded enticingly as she turned around.

Dismissing these unthinkable thoughts, he carried on with his errands and waited for the evening to arrive.

In an unusually cold May, that Saturday night was no exception. The forecast had even threatened a sprinkling of snow. Joan picked him up at 7.30pm as arranged and from the moment George got in, the conversation never stopped. Preparations for university, reminiscences of her own university days and looking to the future were all covered off with great alacrity. He didn't notice the journey milestones and landmarks, so often recognised and counted when on a bike, but here there was only one focus: each other.

Installed comfortably in a secluded corner of a pub close to her workplace at the college, seemed an entirely appropriate location for a drink. Not just because of his impending travel to the far north of the country, which chimed more closely with her own background, but also because of the youthful vigour she injected into the conversation at every point. Her clear but soft, lilting Edinburgh accent caressed his ears, making listening a pleasure. She regaled him with her own stories of adventure, downplayed in her own self-deprecating way, of the time before marriage.

She did not talk of her young son or husband. This was a night of freedom from parental responsibilities when she could return to who she was – a vibrant, animated conversationalist and at the same time an exciting presence. With coats put on the seat next to them, she moved to sit next to George, sitting with a straight deportment which pushed her voluptuous figure into a generous full profile, he felt, for his benefit.

Assuming nothing, the conversation turned to politics and how the colour of political affiliations changes from university days, once house ownership – or rather mortgage indebtedness – takes hold. 'Like every other family, the struggle to meet payments and manage money puts a strain on relationships too', she acknowledged. This was but an isolated moment of foreboding in an otherwise entertaining evening. When she rose to visit the loo and returned to pick up her coat, George felt that it was only right to leave just before half ten, as she would have things she needed to get back to. So he grabbed his donkey jacket and they stepped out into a surprisingly chilly night.

No words were spoken as they crossed the car park to the far side, where her car was parked. The condensation on the windscreen and side windows showed how cold and humid the evening had become.

'I'll just start the car and leave the engine running for a bit. Are you ok?' she asked, concerned that he was discernibly shaking and trying to conceal it by putting his hands together between his thighs, to warm them up or keep them still or both. She sensed the nervous energy between them and asked again in a more protracted manner, 'Are you sure you're ok George?'

'Well,' he said trying to be prosaic, but all the while wondering what might happen next, 'this cold certainly isn't helping things.' With that, she instinctively leaned across to his half of the car and found his mouth with hers and they started to kiss intensely, unleashing pent up undercurrents of feelings which had pervaded their every word of conversation. His hand surprised Joan as much as it did George in its audacious and unplanned movement, when it cupped her full right breast. She broke off their kiss prematurely, which made him think he had been too forward with no clue as to what to do in this position. 'Well, you certainly know what you're doing!' she reassured him encouragingly. Before he knew it they were locked in another, fuller embrace, her tongue searching his mouth, while her right hand moved immediately to his crutch, massaging his manhood in a way entirely and exhilaratingly new. He couldn't help himself and again, in what he thought a total disaster, he ejaculated into his jeans without any rapturous sounds, but mere pent-up frustration at his inability to control such things.

'Well, I'd better get you home I suppose,' she mused, 'but if I had my way, you wouldn't be going home at all!'

He was unsure whether she had noticed the dampening patch on his jeans before he closed the leaves of his jacket about him. Maybe she was just looking for another opportunity to continue what she had started. 'It's not the most private of places', she added, which confirmed his wildest thoughts. Be that as it may, he very much doubted he could summon up the strength to perform again. He had never tried doing that twice in one evening.

As they pulled away from the town and headed out into the country, he now clocked every opening between hedgerows, gathered all his cycling knowledge of the landscape and tried to recollect potential stopping places en route, but came up short. There was an opening at the top of a hill, but that was the Icknield Way, which could attract late walkers. 'That was no good', he thought and dismissed other scant openings with little or no cover as a lost cause. By the time they pulled up outside his house to drop him off, he was resigned that this was the end of the evening. 'Thank you for an amazing evening', he ventured as his foot stepped outside onto the paving at the pond's edge. She gave him a knowing smile and drove quietly off. It was close to midnight.

'Where had the time gone', he wondered, creeping silently around the side of the house, choosing his steps carefully outside and inside the house, so as not to disturb anyone sleeping within. His father was no doubt on early shift the next day, so no worries there, but his mother was a night owl. So he crept in and out of the bathroom to clean up the gooey mess and snuggled down between the cold sheets, pulling the blanket over him before falling into a deep sleep.

The next few days were puzzling. He could tell no one about what happened, couching everything as "having had a nice time" but itching inside to shout out how incredible it and she had been. Perhaps slightly more concerning, was that he did not catch sight of her at the normal dog walking hours she kept previously, as though her normal routine had been totally disrupted.

It must have been five clear days, when he happened upon her in the Bailey quite by chance. She nervously looked behind her to see if anyone had followed her and apologised for her absence. With a wry smile on her face, she confessed, 'He was not happy at all with how late I came back, especially as pubs shut at eleven. He has banned me from going out again in the evening with you or anyone else for that matter.'

'Luckily he has no idea and accepted cautiously that we were just talking, but deep down does not believe it I think. So we'd better keep apart for now.'

This came as a blow to George but he understood her predicament, said as much and added, 'We must make sure you're safe, first and foremost.'

'Here,' she said,' take this.' She pushed a small volume with a purple and grey cover into his hands. It could not have been more than four by six inches and was barely a half inch in thickness. Concealable as it was, he at once cherished this intimate gift, not giving any time to take in the title before thanking her profusely. She prevented him from pocketing it straight away and teased him invitingly, 'Open the cover page.' In a distinctly feminine hand, were both the familiar and the unfamiliar contained: her first name and a different surname. 'That's my maiden name', she revealed, much to the admiration of George, who clutched it to his breast, before putting it into the large side pocket of his jacket. 'I will cherish it always.'

As she moved off past him, they exchanged a final glance to acknowledge what had passed between them, knowing too that this was probably the last time they would see each other. 'Remember,' she repeated a phrase from that memorable evening, 'everything in moderation!'

His heart full to bursting with admiration, he realised for the first time how meaningful and rewarding a relationship with the opposite sex could be – no matter how fleeting the moment enjoyed – as the culmination of a deepening friendship, which he knew he would probably take to his grave.

About the Author

Peter Massam is a writer who captures a moment in time, a location, events or human interactions that have shaped his life and experiences that have been instrumental in managing the journey.

His previous publications are as a poet and technical author. More recently, the Cuz Collection brought together poetry and complementary sketches and images.

The first collection of short sketch poems captures the motivations behind the urge to draw a scene or capture a moment on camera, which sparks observations or symbolises a trend in attitudes or simply celebrates a moment of beauty or an historical event.

The second collection reflects on the plant choices made in a country garden over 11 years and the memories they evoke from child to adulthood.

A technical book began this journey to help two opposite sides value each other's domain for the good of the Customer, highlighting the importance of what was to become a permanent agenda item at board level – Customer Experience.

First Cuz Collection of Poems

> Sketch Poems (2019; Audible 2020)
> ISBN–13: 978–1701299238

Second Cuz Collection of Poems

> Reflections in a Country Garden (2021)
> ISBN–13: 979–8723096103

Customer Experience

> Managing Service Level Quality across Wireless and Fixed Networks (2007)
> ISBN–13: 978–0470848487

Lightning Source UK Ltd.
Milton Keynes UK
UKHW010131230722
406251UK00002B/58